Emmett's Fans
978-1978144286
1978144288
Written by Tracy Cronce and Emmett Cooper
Photographs by Melissa Cooper

Emmett's Fans

By Tracy Cronce
and Emmett Cooper

This is Emmett.

He really likes fans.

He has a hand-held fan.

It is a water spritzer.

It can spray water to cool you.

This fan runs on a battery.

A battery stores energy to power things
like fans and toys.

Now Emmett has a heavy fan.

It oscillates, which means it can

go from side to side.

This fan is portable.

Portable means it can be moved.

This is a cyclone fan.

It sits on the floor.

A cyclone fan is very powerful.

Use it to cool a big room.

Small fans are nice for little spots,

like your desk.

Here is a black fan. It is lightweight and swivels back and forth.

Small cyclone fans are easy to move.

Emmett has a tower fan.

It has buttons on the top.

It also oscillates.

This fan works well for

medium-sized rooms.

Colored buttons are on this fan.

Each button changes how fast

the fan blows.

The fan's neck can also tilt

forward or backward.

The base, or bottom, of this fan

is removeable.

Emmett's fan can change from a desk fan

to a clip-on fan. By squeezing the clip,

the fan will attach to objects.

Most fans run on electricity.

They have cords to plug them in.

Which fan is your favorite?

Made in United States
Orlando, FL
01 March 2022

15297106R00015